of a
r /

The Library of Living and Working in Colonial Times™

A Day in the Life of a Colonial Glassblower

J. L. Branse

The Rosen Publishing Group's
PowerKids Press™
New York

For Jessica, David, Michael, and Sarah

Published in 2002 by The Rosen Publishing Group, Inc.
29 East 21st Street, New York, NY 10010

Copyright © 2002 by The Rosen Publishing Group, Inc.

First Edition

Book Design: Danielle Primiceri
Layout Design: Maria E. Melendez
Project Editor: Frances E. Ruffin

Photo Credits: Cover and title page (18th century glassblower) © The Granger Collection, New York; p. 4 © North Wind Pictures; p. 7 © Historical Picture Archive/CORBIS; p. 8 © Historical Picture Archive/CORBIS; p. 11 © Historical Picture Archive/CORBIS; p. 12 © Historical Picture Archive/CORBIS; p. 15 © North Wind Pictures; p. 16 © Bettmann/CORBIS; p. 19 © Historical Picture Archive/CORBIS; p. 20 © The Granger Collection, New York.

Branse, J. L.
A day in the life of a colonial glassblower / J.L. Branse.- 1st ed.
   p. cm. — (The library of living and working in colonial times)
Includes index.
ISBN 0-8239-5820-5
1. Glass blowing and working–United States–History–18th century–Juvenile literature. [1. Glass blowing and working–History–18th century.] I. Title. II. Series.
TP846.U5 B73 2002
748.2'028'2097309033–dc21   00-012446

Manufactured in the United States of America

Contents

The Glasshouse

On a fall morning in 1740, Karl Berger and his 12-year-old son Fritz left their home to go to the **glasshouse**, or glass factory, where they both worked. The glasshouse was near the city of Philadelphia in the **colony** of Pennsylvania. Karl was a glassblower, a **craftsman** who made bottles, window glass, jars, pitchers, and other objects by blowing air into hot glass through a tube. His son Fritz was an **apprentice**. Karl, his wife Renata, and Fritz had come from Germany to Pennsylvania three years earlier.

◀ *These men are working in a glass factory during the 1800s.*

German Craftsmen

Karl Berger and his son Fritz greeted the other workers at the glasshouse. Karl was one of five glassblowers, and there were other men who performed different jobs at the factory. There were also five other apprentices besides Fritz. Germans were **expert** glassmakers, so most of the other workers were German like Karl and Fritz. The goods that were made at the glasshouse were sold in a shop not far from the factory. **Merchants** in nearby towns also sold them.

The workers in a glasshouse performed many different jobs. ▶

A Successful Business

About 15,000 bottles were made at the glasshouse each year, as well as window glass and other items. It had not been easy for Mr. Bauer, the owner of the glasshouse, to get his business started. He hired experienced workers. He spent money for wood to heat the furnace. He bought clay to build the pots used to melt the glass. It had been worth the struggle. American **colonists** were tired of spending so much money for glass **imported** from England. They were glad to buy the less **expensive** glass made in America.

◀ *Workers made glass in a pot in a hot furnace.*

Building a Clay Pot

A hot furnace was used to melt the **materials** that made glass. These materials were melted in a clay pot that took a long time to build. Karl and other workers would wet old and new clay and stomp on the clay with their feet. Next, they left the clay to ripen, or dry, for six months to a year. Then it was shaped into a pot 3 feet (91 cm) across and 3 feet (91 cm) high. This pot could hold 1,800 pounds (816 kg) of melted glass. Once a pot was shaped, it had to dry for a full year before it was ready to be baked in a **kiln**.

These workers are making a clay pot. ▶

Melting Glass

All glass is made of sand that is melted at a high temperature. Today we know that it takes temperatures from 2,300 to 2,700 degrees **Fahrenheit** (1,260 –1,482 °C) to melt sand into glass. Different materials are added to make colored glass. The furnace where Karl worked was large and circular. The pot that would hold sand was heated for one week so that it would be the same temperature as the furnace.

◀ *Materials used to make glass were added to the pot through a hole in the furnace wall.*

Blowing Glass

Karl reached for his most important tool, a 6-foot (1.8-m) iron tube called a blowing iron. The blowing iron had a wooden handle and a wooden mouthpiece. Karl dipped the blowing iron into the pot that held the hot glass. He took out a melted blob of hot glass called a parison. Before Karl blew the parison, he made sure it was even on all sides by rolling it on an iron table. Then he blew into the blowing tube to make the parison into a bubble that was the right size for the glass bottle he was making.

Hot glass was heavy and thick. Sometimes glassblowers would inhale hot air, which hurt their lungs. ▶

Passing the Bottle

Karl blew a green glass bottle to just the right size. The neck end of the bottle was attached to the blowing iron. His son Fritz, who was one of the apprentices, came over with an iron rod called a punty. At the end of the punty was a small bit of hot glass. The hot glass made the punty stick to the bottom of the bottle that Karl had just blown. Then another workman used a drop of water to break the hot glass bottle's neck from the blowing iron. Fritz turned the punty straight up with the bottom of the bottle attached to it.

◀ *Apprentices, like Karl's son Fritz, were careful in their work, and they worked hard.*

The Gaffer

Karl's friend August Newmann was a gaffer. A gaffer helped to shape a bottle or an object after it was blown. August sat in a chair that had iron covering its arms. This **protected** the arms of the chair from the hot glass. The tools August needed to finish a piece of glasswork hung from pegs on the chair. August sat close to the furnace so that he could reheat any glass that started to harden as it cooled. If the glass cooled too much, August could no longer shape it the way that he wanted.

These images show gaffers shaping glass. ▶

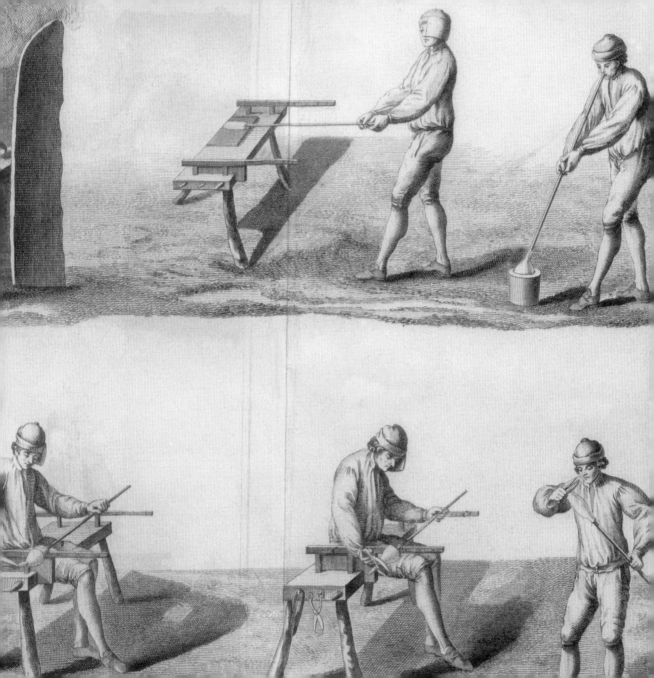

Finishing a Bottle

The first thing August Newmann, a gaffer, did when he got the bottle was to give the punty a gentle push. This made a small dent on the bottom of the bottle. The dent on the bottom was what made the bottle stand once it was finished. Then August made a band around the neck of the bottle. He used a different tool to make the neck look neat and to make a place on the inside of the bottle for a cork to fit. Karl smiled and told his friend that he had done a good job.

◀ *This English wine decanter and these lead-glass dishes were made in 1675.*

The Leer

Glass has to be cooled slowly or it becomes **brittle** and breaks. To prevent this, glasshouses built long, brick tunnels called leers. As the glass went through the leer, it moved farther away from the heat. At the far end of the leer, the glass came out cool and strong. Karl stood at the cool end of the leer and watched a tray of glass bottles come out. He could always tell which bottles he had blown. He was proud of his skill as a glassblower. He was proud of the life he had built for himself and his family in America, too.

Glossary

apprentice (uh-PREN-tis) An inexperienced person learning a skill or trade.

brittle (BRIH-tul) Easily broken.

colonists (KAH-luh-nists) People who live in a colony.

colony (KAH-luh-nee) An area in a new country where a large group of people move who are still ruled by the leaders and laws of their old country.

craftsman (KRAFTS-man) A workman who practices a certain trade.

expensive (ek-SPEN-siv) Costing a lot of money.

expert (EK-spert) Knowing a lot about a subject.

Fahrenheit (FEHR-un-hyt) A temperature scale that measures the freezing point of water as 32 degrees and the boiling point as 212 degrees.

glasshouse (GLAS-hows) A factory in colonial America where glass objects were made.

imported (im-POR-tid) Brought from another country for sale or use.

kiln (KILN) An oven used to dry clay.

materials (muh-TIR-ee-ulz) The things from which objects are made.

merchants (MUR-chints) People who sell things.

protected (pruh-TEK-tid) To have kept from harm.

Index

Web Sites:

To learn more about glassblowing, check out these Web sites:

www.cmog.org

www.eng.iastate.edu/explorer/glassblowing/
    glassblowing.htm